21st-century SCIENCE

MEDICINE

Present knowledge • Future trends

Written by Robin Kerrod

W

FRANKLIN WATTS
LONDON • SYDNEY

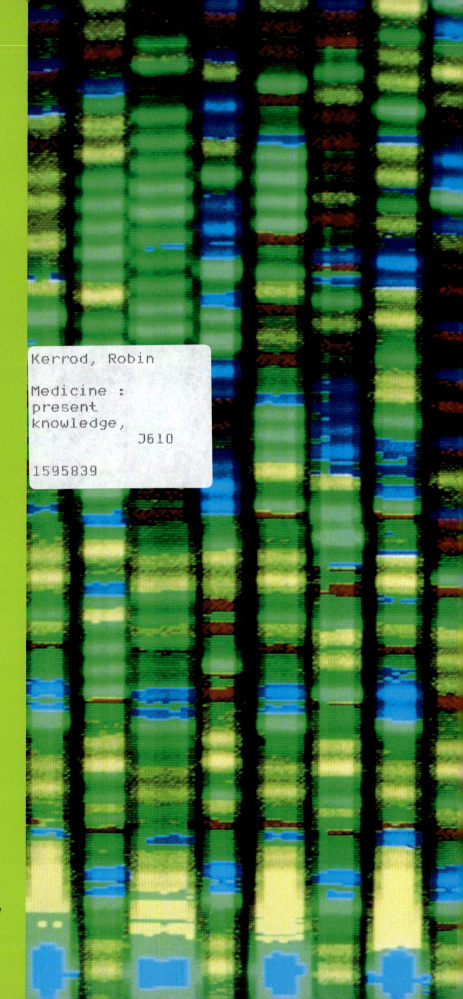

First published
in 2004 by

Franklin Watts
96 Leonard Street
London EC2A 4XD

Franklin Watts Australia
45-51 Huntley Street
Alexandria
NSW 2015

Design Billin Design Solutions
Editors Constance Novis, Sarah Ridley
Art Director Jonathan Hair
Editor-in-Chief John C. Miles
Picture Research Diana Morris

A CIP catalogue record for this book
is available from the British Library.

ISBN 0 7496 5385 X

Printed in Hong Kong, China

Picture credits
Samuel Ashfield/SPL: 27
BSIP/Edwidge/SPL: 32
BSIP/Laurent/Dr Gaillard/SPL:front cover bc,
31
Mark Clarke/SPL: 13
CNRI/SPL: 23b
Deep Light/SPL: front cover t
Simon Fraser/SPL: 4-5, 10, 20tr, 30
Russell Kightley/SPL: front cover br, 16
Robin Laurance/SPL: 21b
Matt Meadows/Peter Arnold, Inc/SPL: 26t
Peter Menzel/SPL: 33
Dr Gopal Murti/SPL: 15, 45, back endpapers
NASA: 40, 41
National Cancer Institute/SPL: front cover c,
back cover background, 11, 20bl
Steve Patterson/SPL: 14
Phillipe Plailly/Eurelios/SPL: 6-7, 9b, 34, 35, 38
W. A. Ritchie/Roslin Institute/Eurelios/SPL: 39
Professor K Seddon & Dr T Evans, Queens
University, Belfast/SPL: 25
Blair Seitz/SPL: 12t
Sinclair Stammers/SPL: 17
SIU/Peter Arnold Inc/SPL: front endpapers, 24
Volker Steger/SPL: 37
Sheila Terry/SPL: 19
Mark Thomas/SPL: 28, 29
Zephyr/SPL: front cover br, 8t

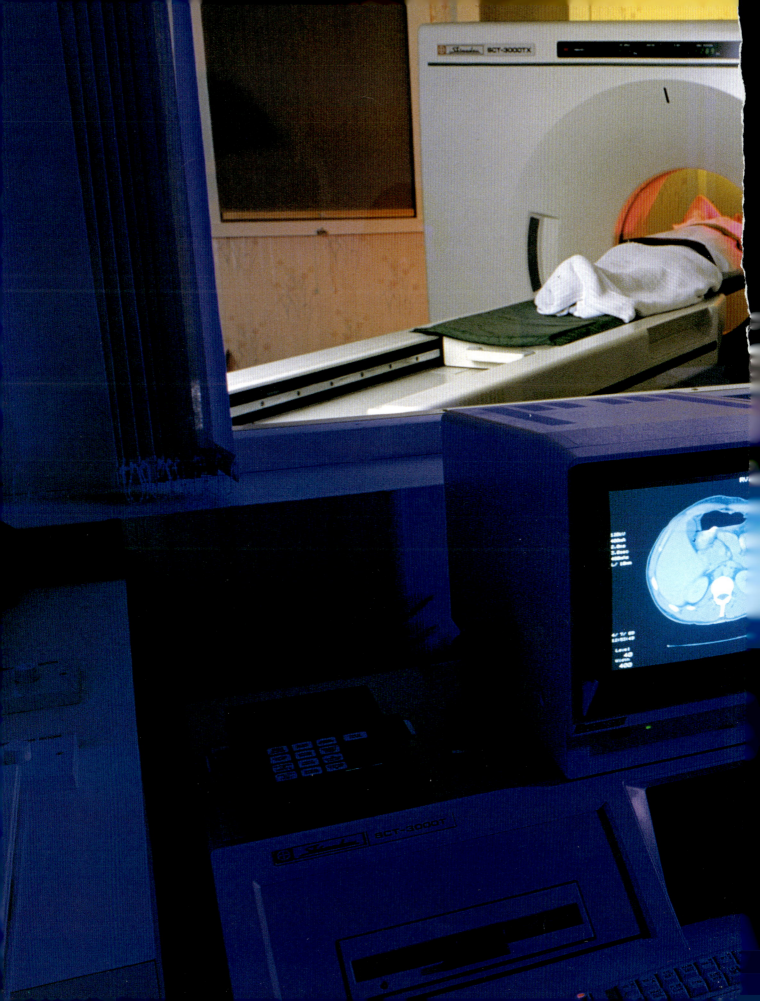

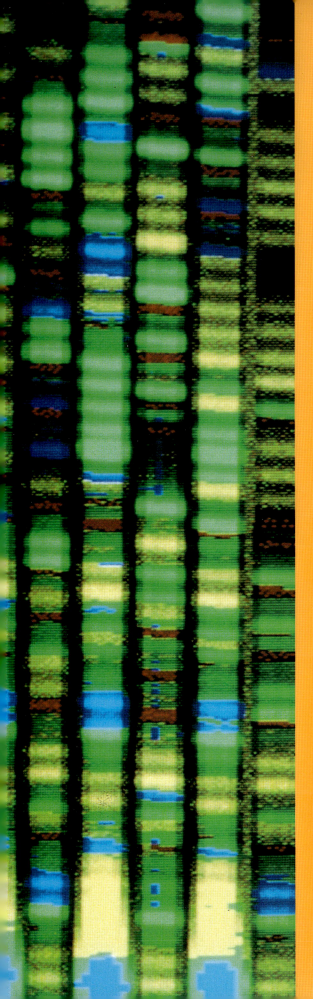

Contents

Introduction

In the 21st century, medicine has become one of the most exciting branches of science. This is an era of designer drugs and organ transplants, of spare-part surgery and diagnostic scanners. But the biggest growth area is genetics, especially since the completion of the Human Genome Project.

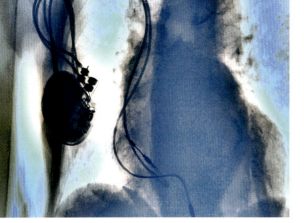

▲

Modern medicine can treat many different ailments. This coloured X-ray image shows a heart pacemaker implanted in the chest of a patient.

Medicine has a long history, with origins in early civilisations. Ancient Egyptian wall paintings at Memphis dating from about 2500BC show pictures of surgical operations. The ancient Chinese were experimenting with potions and medicinal plants around this time too.

Western medicine has its roots in the work and teachings of Hippocrates of ancient Greece. He lived from about 460BC to about 377BC and is known as the father of medicine. He established the famed Hippocratic Oath, a universally recognised code of medical conduct.

Foundations of medicine

However, it was not until the Renaissance in Europe, more than a thousand years later, that the science of medicine blossomed. In the 1500s, a Belgian named Andreas Vesalius (1514-1564) used careful dissection of the human body to found the science of anatomy. The Englishman William Harvey (1578-1657) demonstrated the circulation of the blood in the 1600s. Around this time the Dutch naturalist Anton von Leeuwenhoek (1632-1723) pioneered the use of the microscope.

In the late 1700s, the English physician Edward Jenner (1749-1823) performed the first vaccinations against smallpox, introducing the principle of mass protection against infectious diseases. In the next century, Frenchman Louis Pasteur (1822-1895) and German Robert Koch (1843-1910) established bacteria as the cause of many infections. And the

German physicist Wilhelm Röntgen (1845-1923) discovered X-rays, which were to become one of medicine's most vital diagnostic tools.

Fighting infection

By the end of the 1800s, the effectiveness of aspirin as a painkiller had been demonstrated, and it soon became the world's most widely used drug. In the 1930s, German bacteriologist Gerhard Domagk (1895-1964) discovered synthetic chemicals called sulphonamides, which formed the basis of powerful sulpha drugs that could treat and cure a wide range of illnesses. They dramatically cut the death rate from diseases like pneumonia and meningitis that were, until then, scarcely treatable.

In the 1940s, the first antibiotic, penicillin, came into use, pioneering the now preferred treatment of a wide spectrum of illnesses, from sore throats and boils to whooping cough and tuberculosis.

In 1953, Francis Crick (1916-) and James Watson (1928-) unravelled the structure of DNA and established genetics as the science of the future. The year 1960 saw the launch of the birth-control pill, and 1967 the first heart transplant. In 1978, Louise Brown became the first test-tube baby. And by the dawn of the new millennium, the first draft of the human genome had been published.

Proceed with caution

While medical science is progressing in leaps and bounds on many fronts, worrying problems still remain. For example, the widespread use of antibiotics has led to the evolution of new generations of 'superbugs', which are resistant to antibiotics.

In highly developed countries, over-eating has caused obesity to become a leading 'disease' – 60 per cent of Americans, for example, are overweight. Meanwhile, in developing countries, malnutrition, coupled with lack of clean water and poor health care, is a killer. More than 10 million children are dying before they reach the age of five.

And the progress in genetics is becoming increasingly controversial. It is raising questions about the ethics of tampering with human cells and embryos, and 'creating' genetically altered human beings.

▼

The blueprint of life: this coloured image shows part of the sequencing of human DNA.

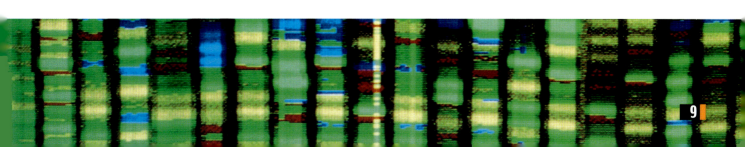

THE LIVING MACHINE

The marvellous organism that is the human body is the result of millions of years of evolution. It is a collection of as many as 50 million million cells, organised into different systems that give it structure and make it work.

The framework

The body is built around a sturdy framework, the skeleton, which gives the body its shape and also protects vital organs like the brain and heart. The skeleton is clothed in flesh, with an outer covering of waterproof skin. With an area of about 2 square metres (21 square feet), the skin is in fact the largest 'organ' of the body.

The skeleton is made up of about 206 bones, most linked together by flexible joints. Some 600 muscles attached to the bones allow movement around the joints. Muscle tissue makes up around 40 per cent of total body weight.

Circulation and respiration

The cells in all parts of the body are kept alive by the blood that flows to them via a complex network of tubes, or vessels. Arteries and veins are the primary blood vessels, thin capillaries the smallest ones. The blood carries food and other nutrients to the cells and removes waste products from them.

Beating around 70 times a minute, the heart is the pump

hat circulates the blood. It handles two circulation systems. One system carries blood to and from the lungs. The other carries it to other parts of the body.

The blood also transports oxygen, which cells need to 'burn' the food to make energy. Oxygen from the air passes into the blood in the lungs when we breathe in. At the same time, carbon dioxide waste in the blood passes back into the air, which we breathe out. We call this constant exchange of gases in the lungs respiration.

Digestion and excretion

Food is taken in and processed by the digestive system, made up of what is essentially a long tube. The digestion process starts with the action of saliva in the mouth and continues by the action of digestive juices in the stomach.

The food being digested passes into the upper part of the small intestine, where it is mixed with digestive juices from the pancreas and gall bladder. Gradually, as the food moves along, nutrients flow from it through the intestine walls into the bloodstream. The indigestible part of the food eventually enters the large intestine, or colon, which rids it of excess water. The solid waste exits the body through the anus.

Control systems

The nervous system exercises strict control over all the body's activities under the direction of a 'supercomputer' – the brain. Messages to and from the brain travel via an intricate network of nerves. The main 'route' for travel is the spinal cord, through which signals race at lightning speed as electrical impulses.

Specialised parts of the nervous system are known as the sense organs and include the eyes, ears and nose. These organs feed information to the brain about the world around us.

Chemicals can also exercise control and carry messages around the body. The chemical messengers, called hormones, are made in glands. Adrenal glands make adrenaline and they pour out the hormone at times of stress when the body needs to act quickly. The pancreas makes insulin, which the body needs to break down sugars.

◄ ◄

A coloured MRI (magnetic resonance imaging) scan of the front of a woman shows many of her body structures.

▼

A magnified view of the main components of blood - red and white blood cells.

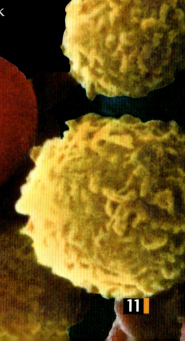

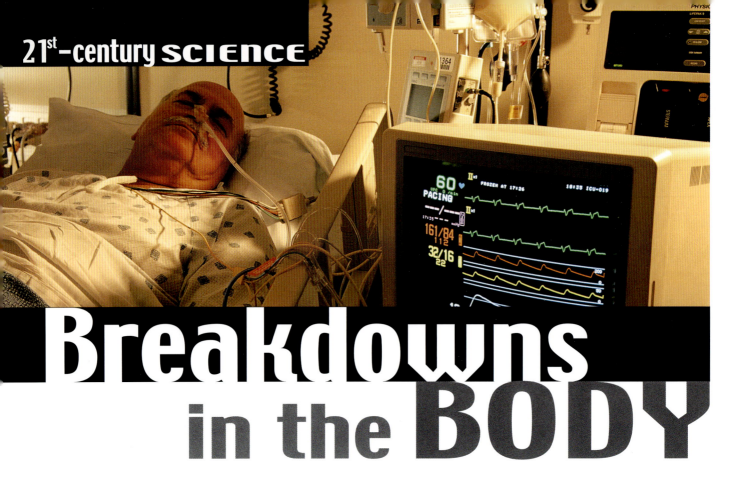

Breakdowns in the BODY

People become ill when something goes wrong with their organs or body systems. Sometimes this occurs as a result of the genes they inherited from their parents. Here are just a few common disorders which may, or may not, be life-threatening.

▲

This view of a modern cardiac intensive care unit shows a patient linked up to a nasal tube, intravenous drips and a vital signs monitor on the right.

Heart attacks

One of the biggest killers is heart disease, which can lead to heart attacks, or coronaries. They occur because of narrowing or complete blockage of the coronary arteries that feed oxygen-rich blood to the heart muscles. This prevents the heart from beating properly, which interrupts blood supply to the brain. Death results if this blood supply is cut off for too long.

A natural build-up of material around artery walls occurs as a person ages. But this build-up, called arteriosclerosis, can be accelerated by an unhealthy life-style of eating fatty, high-cholesterol foods, smoking and not getting enough exercise.

Digestive disorders

By far the commonest problem is the inflammation of the most useless part of the intestinal tract – the appendix – which plays no part in digestion. If a diseased appendix tears or splits open, toxic substances are released that cause peritonitis, which can be fatal.

Painful ulcers may occur in the stomach and in the duodenum, the upper part of the small intestine. Known as peptic ulcers, they can be brought on by stress, eating an unhealthy diet and drinking too much alcohol.

Colitis, an inflammation of the large intestine, or colon, can also be linked to poor diet and too much stress. Small growths, or polyps, sometimes occur in the colon. Some may eventually develop into tumours, causing bowel cancer.

Hormonal problems

One of the most common hormonal problems affecting people is caused by the malfunction of the pancreas. The job of the pancreas is to produce the hormone insulin, designed to break down sugars. If the pancreas malfunctions, not enough insulin is produced and sugar builds up in the blood. Untreated, this condition can lead to problems with the circulation and eyes, and damage to the kidneys.

The pituitary gland produces growth hormone. Sometimes it does not produce enough, which leads to dwarfism. Sometimes it produces too much, leading to gigantism. Changes in the sex hormones of women at the end of their reproductive life bring on the menopause, with a variety of symptoms, from hot flushes to depression.

Nervous system

The nervous system can suffer too, either from accidental damage, infection or other causes. Damage to the spinal column can lead to partial or nearly complete paralysis. A number of people suffer from epilepsy, experiencing periodic fits of uncontrolled shaking, triggered by violent electrical activity in the brain.

Wasting diseases also take their toll. They include motor neurone disease, multiple sclerosis and Parkinson's disease. Senile dementia and Alzheimer's disease are degenerative brain disorders that may develop, usually late in life.

▼

Some people suffering from diabetes need to inject themselves with the vital hormone insulin.

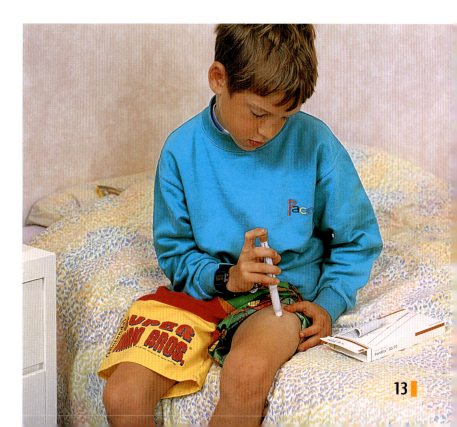

13

THE BODY under attack

The human body is under constant attack from the outside too, and even the healthiest people can have accidents. But it is attack by the smallest living organisms – bacteria and viruses – that wreak the most havoc on the body. Pests and pollution also take their toll.

Bacteria

Bacteria are by far the most numerous life forms on Earth. Whereas there are only about 6,000 million people on our planet, there are estimated to be five million million million million million bacteria.

Fortunately, only a few kinds are actually harmful to human beings. Some are even beneficial. For example, some bacteria help enrich the soil by bringing about the decay of dead animal and plant material. Other bacteria are used to make yoghurt and cheese.

But what exactly is a bacterium? It is a microscopic organism about a thousand times smaller than a typical human cell. And it differs from human and animal cells because it does not have a central nucleus.

Deadly divisions

Bacteria can enter the body via the air you breathe or through cuts and abrasions on the skin. Most kinds get mopped up by the body's natural defences (see page 20). But some do not.

By feeding on the blood or body tissue, they can divide and multiply at an alarming rate – a single bacterium might produce billions of offspring in just a day. Reproducing at this rate, they can overwhelm the body's defences. They cause illness by attacking body tissue and also by producing poisonous toxins.

Bacterial diseases

Among the many diseases bacteria cause are cholera, diphtheria, food poisoning, leprosy, pneumonia,

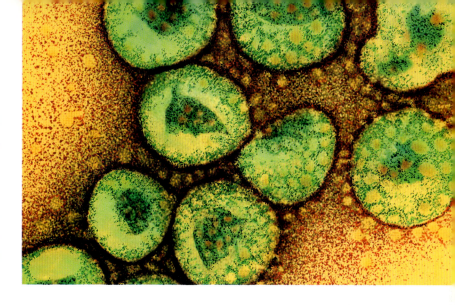

tetanus, tuberculosis, typhoid and whooping cough. With pneumonia (which can also be caused by viruses), the lungs become painfully inflamed, making breathing difficult. A particularly deadly strain is Legionnaires' disease, which claimed 29 lives of the 182 people affected in the first known outbreak in 1976. Tuberculosis (TB) is another debilitating lung disease, which is on the increase again (see page 24).

A number of bacteria cause food poisoning. Staphylococci and Salmonella cause many outbreaks. Thankfully rare, poisoning by *Clostridium botulinum* causes botulism, creating toxins that can bring on paralysis and death. Another Clostridium (C.) bacterium, *C. tetani*, is found widely in the soil. It produces toxins that attack nerves, causing lockjaw, for example.

Vicious viruses

Viruses are even smaller than bacteria and can be equally deadly. A virus is a tiny protein 'package' containing a strand of DNA (see page 34).

Viruses are organisms that seem to lie on the border between living and non-living things. They cannot reproduce by themsleves.

A virus can reproduce only within the cells of other organisms. But when it gets in, it takes over the host cell and directs it to produce more viruses, which go on to attack more cells. In this way, viruses quickly ravage their host's body.

Viral infections

Among the diseases caused by viruses are chickenpox, hepatitis A and B, influenza, mumps, poliomyelitis, measles and rubella (German measles). AIDS is a particularly nasty viral disease that affects the body's immune system (see page 21).

However, the most frequently seen viral infection by far is the common cold, which affects many millions of people throughout the world every year.

Colds are caused by what are called coronaviruses, which target the respiratory tract and cause a runny nose, inflamed membranes and sore throat. Usually these viruses do little more than cause discomfort for a few days.

▲

A coloured view through an electron microscope of the coronavirus which causes the common cold in humans.

◀ ◀

Another view of coronaviruses. Like all viruses, the coronavirus infects a host cell in order to reproduce itself.

THE BODY under attack

▲

A highly magnified view of the type of coronavirus thought to cause SARS.

people appear to spread the infection faster than others. Just a single 'superspreader' is believed to have triggered an outbreak in Toronto that affected 250 people and killed 38.

New strains of influenza ('flu) viruses also regularly spring up and affect millions. The elderly, whose ability to fight off illnesses may be weak, are particularly at risk from the infections. In the great Spanish 'flu pandemic (worldwide epidemic) of 1918-19, as many as 20 million people died in 18 months.

Deadly SARS

However, late in 2002, a deadly strain of the coronavirus appeared in China and quickly spread around the world, causing SARS, or severe acute respiratory syndrome. By July 2003, SARS had affected more than 8,400 people and killed 813.

SARS victims suffer fever, headaches and an aching body and have difficulty breathing. SARS spreads like wildfire, through close contact, coughs and sneezes, or touching contaminated objects. Some

Pests and parasites

The body suffers not only from the invisible menace of microbes, but from more tangible attackers, such as ants, bees, wasps and mosquitoes, which sting and bite.

Mosquito bites can be the most dangerous. Only female mosquitoes bite – and they do so to suck blood. If the blood they suck is infected, they carry that infection to the next victim they bite, animal or human.

Mosquitoes are responsible for the spread of yellow fever and malaria. Yellow fever is caused by a virus and malaria is caused by protozoans (simple single-celled life forms) called Plasmodia. Several species of Anopheles mosquitoes can transmit these organisms. Malaria is still one of the world's most widespread illnesses, marked by chills, fevers and general weakness. Every year, there are up to 500 million cases of malaria around the world, and as many as 2.5 million people die.

Pollution

A variety of other agents in the environment can also threaten the body. For example, in modern intensive agriculture, pesticides and other chemicals are used routinely to protect crops and livestock from insect pests, fungal infections, invading weeds and so on.

It is reckoned that a supermarket apple, for example, may have been treated up to 40 times with any of a hundred chemicals. Minute traces of the chemicals may remain in the fruit afterwards but rigorous testing by food standards agencies ensures that levels remain below safety limits.

Polluted air can trigger a range of respiratory illnesses, such as bronchitis, in which the airways, or bronchi, lose their natural resistance and succumb to infections. Smog in big cities, brought on by vehicle fumes, can be a killer. So can fumes released by industrial accidents. In Bhopal, India, in 1984, over 2,000 people were killed and 50,000 others affected when deadly gas was released from a pesticides plant.

Radiation is another potential hazard. Too much ultraviolet radiation from the Sun can cause severe burns. X-rays can be damaging too – but in controlled amounts they have many medical uses (see page 31). Radioactive substances used in the nuclear power industry pose a problem if they escape into the environment. Their penetrating radiation carries a hidden risk because it can cause alterations (mutations) in the body's genes and so affect future generations.

▼

A close-up view of a female Anopheles mosquito feeding. Mosquitoes spread yellow fever, malaria and other diseases.

fighting back

When bacteria, viruses and other organisms attack, the body's own defence system leaps into action. But it often needs help. Over the centuries many substances have been used to help the body to fight off all kinds of illnesses. At first, these drugs were made mainly from plants, and some still are. But most drugs today are man-made.

In tropical South America, the native population have known for a long time how they can help cure the fever they sometimes suffer from. They chew the bark of the cinchona tree. The bark contains quinine, a potent drug for treating malaria, which causes the fever. Like most other drugs, quinine and its derivatives are now produced synthetically from chemicals.

However, a few drugs are still produced from natural sources. Digitalis, used to treat heart conditions, is extracted from a plant called the foxglove. The powerful painkiller morphine is produced from certain poppies. Morphine works by

blocking pain receptors in the brain and so it is classed as a narcotic. Some other common types of drugs are given in the table opposite.

Side effects

Drugs are usually developed for a specific purpose, but they may affect the body in other ways as well. Such side effects can sometimes be harmful. Morphine, for example, is an excellent painkiller, but often induces nightmare-like dreams. It is also highly addictive, which means that the body can become dependent on the drug and develop powerful cravings for it. The same goes for heroin and cocaine. The abuse of

▶ ▶

The foxglove plant is the source of the drug digitalis, used to treat heart conditions.

these and other addictive 'illegal' drugs has led to major social and health problems in many countries.

People can also get addicted to drugs prescribed for routine medical treatment, particularly anti-depressants and tranquillisers. Such people tend to become dependent on the drugs in order to lead 'normal' lives and can suffer severe withdrawal symptoms when they are taken off the drugs.

The scourge of thalidomide

Some side effects can be devastating. In the 1950s, the drug thalidomide was found to be an excellent treatment for morning sickness in pregnant women, and by the end of the decade was being widely prescribed. But it proved to have terrible side effects, causing deformities in the unborn child. More than 5,000 babies were born with ill-formed limbs or organ defects before the drug was banned in 1962.

However, some 40 years later, this drug re-surfaced as a possible treatment for some of the most deadly forms of cancer – of the lung and pancreas – and even HIV, the virus that causes AIDS. It seems to make the body's immune system more effective in coping with abnormalities and invading organisms.

COMMON TYPES OF DRUGS

Drug	What it does
Anaesthetic	Local anaesthetic temporarily deadens sensation in flesh locally; general anaesthetic produces temporary loss of consciousness
Analgesic	Reduces or prevents pain
Antacid	Reduces acidity in the stomach
Antibiotic	Kills bacteria
Anticoagulant	Thins blood to help prevent clotting
Anti-depressant	Relieves depression
Antihistamine	Relieves symptoms of allergies, like hay fever
Anti-inflammatory	Reduces inflammation (swelling) and relieves pain
Antiseptic	Kills germs
Beta-blocker	Helps restore normal heart rhythms
Decongestants	Unblocks sinuses
Diuretic	Improves flow of urine
Hormone	Helps restore hormone levels
Laxative	Makes bowel movements easier
Narcotic	Powerful pain reliever
Sedative	Soothes the body; helps induce sleep
Tranquilliser	Helps treat anxiety and insomnia
Vaccine	Helps build up immunity to disease

21st-century SCIENCE

fighting back

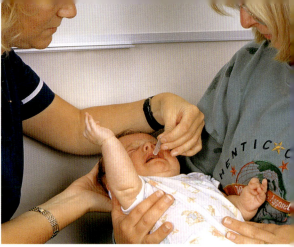

Repelling invaders

This magnified view shows white blood cells (yellow spheres) among red blood cells. White blood cells are part of the body's immune system.

The body's immune system provides a natural defence against invading germs when they get into the body through the nose or mouth or through cuts in the skin. The main players in the system are the white blood cells, which are produced in the bone marrow.

There are two types of cells, lymphocytes and the larger macrophages. The lymphocytes make chemicals called antibodies. These recognise invading 'foreign' organisms and attack them. The macrophages engulf the dead and dying organisms and slowly digest them. Some antibodies remain, and so-called 'memory cells' remember the invasion and trigger further antibody production if the same foreign organism invades again. In this way, the body builds up its own natural immune system.

Immunisation

Doctors take advantage of the memory process to prepare the body to fight some of the most serious diseases we know. The process is known as immunisation because it gives immunity against diseases.

Tiny amounts of weakened or dead bacterium or virus are introduced into the body, usually by an injection.

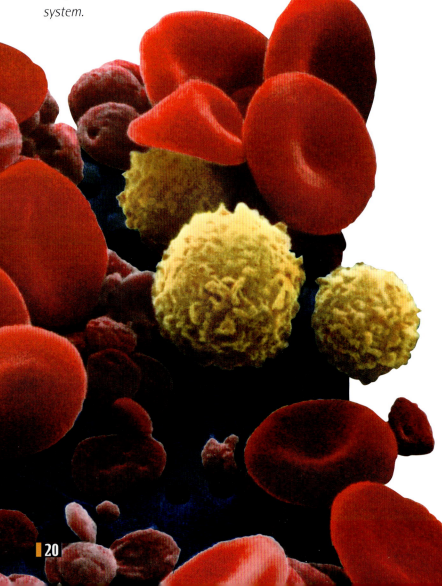

The white cells move in to attack and produce antibodies and memory cells. If a similar active bacterium or virus enters the body in the future, the antibodies will recognise it. This will trigger massive antibody production and the invading illness will be quickly killed.

Vaccines

In 1796, the English physician Edward Jenner (1749-1823) used an injection to prevent smallpox. He discovered that fluids from the spots of people suffering from cowpox could be used to protect against the more serious disease of smallpox. So vaccines take their name from the latin word for cow, *vacca*. A mass immunisation campaign eradicated smallpox as a disease in 1977.

Today, young children are routinely given vaccines to guard against diseases like polio, diphtheria, whooping cough and measles. Vaccines are so far the most effective way of dealing with viruses. But more and more antiviral drugs, such as interferon, are coming into use. However, these inhibit virus growth – they do not bring about a cure.

Destroying immunity

No vaccine is available yet to combat one of the most devastating diseases known – AIDS, or acquired immune deficiency syndrome. The virus, HIV, or human immunodeficiency virus, causes AIDS by destroying the body's immune system, leaving the body defenceless against all kinds of infections. HIV can be spread through sexual contact and contaminated blood.

People infected with HIV may remain outwardly healthy for years, then many will go on to develop full-blown AIDS. Treatment with antiviral drugs like AZT (zidovudine) may help combat the infection.

AIDS first became recognised as a problem in 1981. By the end of 2002, it was estimated that more than 40 million people in the world suffered from AIDS or were infected with HIV. Three million people died of AIDS that year, bringing the total death toll since the epidemic began to more than 17 million.

◄ ◄

A nurse gives oral polio vaccine to a three-month-old baby boy.

▼

Medical researchers develop new vaccines in laboratories.

Battling bacteria

The battle against bacteria is much more successful than that against viruses. Chemicals called antibiotics are used to kill bacteria. But they have been used so widely that bacteria are now evolving that resist antibiotic action. Perhaps the ultimate answer lies in so-called 'designer drugs' based on the life molecule itself, DNA.

The British bacteriologist Alexander Fleming (1855-1955) discovered the first antibiotic in 1928. He noticed that a substance produced by a Penicillium mould killed surrounding germs, so he called it penicillin.

But it was not until 1940 that two other British scientists, Howard Florey (1898-1968) and Ernst Chain (1906-1979), purified penicillin and established its outstanding effectiveness against disease. By 1945, penicillin was being produced in quantity and was used with spectacular success in treating infections among the wounded soldiers of World War II.

Penicillin's success prompted the search for other micro-organisms that had antibiotic action. Hundreds have been found but relatively few have proved clinically useful. Many kill bacteria but are also toxic to humans.

Producing antibiotics

Most antibiotics are derived from bacteria that live in the soil, particularly the Streptomyces (S.) species. It was from *S. griseus* that the second antibiotic, streptomycin, was produced. Tetracycline is another powerful Streptomyces antibiotic.

The standard method of producing antibiotics is a mass-production version of the way bacteria are grown in the laboratory. They are grown in a so-called culture medium, which provides suitable nutrients and conditions for micro-organisms to grow. On the industrial scale, production takes place in huge fermentation vessels. The culture is stirred continuously as air bubbles through it, and the micro-organisms grow throughout the medium rather than just at the surface.

Antibiotic action

Antibiotics work in two main ways. Some prevent bacteria from making their cell walls. The internal contents of the cells are lost, and the bacteria die. Penicillin and related antibiotics, such as ampicillin and methicillin, act like this.

Other antibiotics work by interfering with the process by which bacteria synthesise (produce) proteins. And if they can't produce proteins, they can't reproduce. Among the many antibiotics that work by interfering with protein synthesis are

erythromycin, streptomycin and tetracycline. Tetracycline is known as a broad-spectrum antibiotic because it can be used to target many diseases.

Putting up resistance

Bacteria have been around for at least 3,000 million years. So it is perhaps no surprise that they do not stand idly by to be slaughtered. Subtly they alter and start to become resistant to antibiotic action. This process is typical of the way evolution works.

Antibiotic resistance is growing rapidly because of the widespread use of antibiotics not only for treating human illnesses but animals as well. They are routinely used in modern intensive farming to prevent disease and improve growth. We absorb animal antibiotics when we eat meat or animal products.

▼

This hugely magnified image shows the effect of antibiotics on bacteria. The bacterium on the left has been destroyed; the one on the right is, as yet, undamaged.

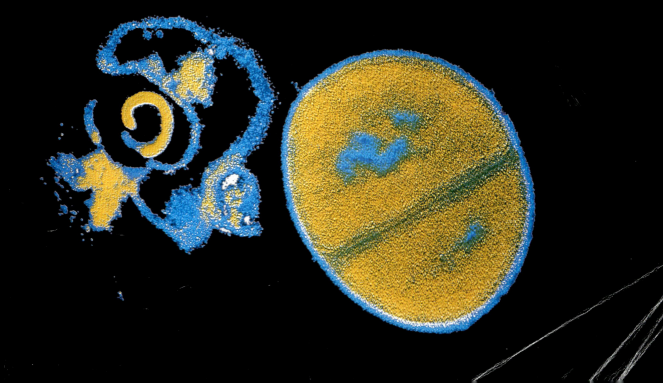

Battling bacteria

The superbugs

Increasing antibiotic resistance is leading to the appearance of new 'superbugs', particularly in hospitals. One of the major culprits is MRSA, methicillin-resistant *Staphylococcus aureus*. Antibiotic resistance is also leading to a resurgence in tuberculosis (TB). Cases of MDR-TB (multiple drug-resistant TB) are rising alarmingly. By 2002, London was seeing 50 new cases a week; Romania was reporting over 100 cases for every 100,000 people.

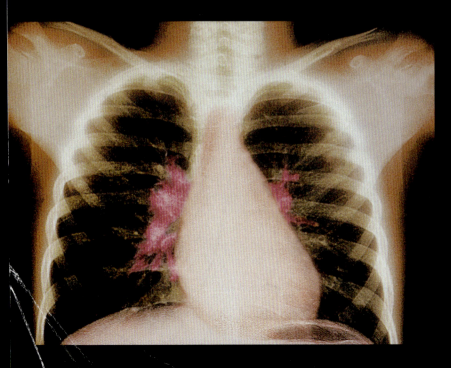

A coloured X-ray image of the lungs of a person with TB. The areas of the lungs affected by the disease are shown in pink.

Back to the future

The emergence of resistant strains of bacteria is threatening a Dark Age in medicine, unless new antibiotics are discovered. But all bacteria will in time probably become resistant to them too.

One solution may be to use organisms called bacteriophages (bacteria killers) to fight bacterial infection. Phages were first discovered in 1915. They are a kind of virus that attacks bacteria and forces them to produce new viruses, destroying them in the process. They are much bigger than ordinary viruses. The most common kind is distinctive, with a shaped head and a tail with fibres attached.

Early research suggested that phages could be used to fight disease, but in most countries work on phages virtually ceased after the discovery of antibiotics. But it continued in Russia and other eastern European countries, where phage treatment has been practised.

Research on phages is now underway in many other countries to try to produce phages to combat

infection from antibiotic-resistant bacteria like *Staphylococcus aureus*. The matter is becoming urgent.

Designer drugs

Another approach to finding more effective treatments for diseases is to create better drugs. Drug designers use the latest cutting-edge technologies – electron microscopes, immensely powerful computers and robots – and the latest data about the genetic make-up of the human body.

They can create models on a computer that show the structures of organisms, such as viruses. The computer can then help design possible vaccines to combat them, making sure they have the right shape to fit around the virus molecules, enabling the vaccine to interfere with their action. The computer can simulate this.

In the genes

Drug designers are also turning to the genes in DNA to design new products. They can find the genetic make-up of the substances that cause medical problems (often proteins) and produce drugs that more accurately inhibit their action.

The direct injection of genetic material into tissues is another novel approach in treatment, and it is currently being used to treat heart conditions. Hundreds of thousands of people a year suffer heart trouble because their hearts do not get a good enough blood supply. This can usually be corrected by surgery.

But a 'genetic' approach is proving successful. The growth-factor gene is injected directly into heart muscle. It stimulates the growth of new blood vessels, which then deliver the extra oxygen to the heart.

▲

Not all 'designer' drugs are medically useful. This is a computer model of the chemical structure of the drug Ecstasy. The recreational use of this drug has caused many deaths.

Coping with CANCER

Cancer is one of the world's biggest killers, affecting millions of people around the world every year. It is not one disease but many, which can target almost any part of the body. But many cancers can be treated successfully if they are caught early enough.

▲

This picture shows a patient with a brain tumour about to undergo radiotherapy, in which a beam of radiation is directed at the tumour in order to shrink it.

In a normal healthy body, the cells replace themselves on a routine basis. Cancer occurs when something goes wrong with this replacement process and abnormal cells are produced. These cells divide much more rapidly than normal cells and form growths, called tumours. If the tumours grow big enough, they can overwhelm the body and may cause death.

Kinds of cancers

Parts of the body that commonly succumb to cancers are the lungs, colon and liver. In women the breast and cervix can become cancerous and in men the prostate. Leukaemia is a cancer of the blood, and malignant melanoma is a cancer of the skin. All of them are potential killers.

Cancer cells do not grow rapidly in just one place. They may also migrate in the blood, passing through the lymph system to other parts of the body, where they establish secondary growths, or metastases. Metastases from colon cancer, for example, commonly occur in the liver.

Statistically, lung cancer is the most common kind, killing one person somewhere in the world every 30 seconds. Ironically, it is the most preventable of cancers, being caused primarily by cigarette smoking.

After lung cancer, colorectal cancer – cancer of the colon and rectum – is the biggest killer. Nearly 450,000 people die of the disease every year around the world. The good news is that this is one of the more easily curable cancers, provided it can be caught early enough.

Cancer screening

Almost all cancers are treatable, though not necessarily curable, if they are diagnosed early enough. Methods of detecting cancers are now quite sophisticated.

Cervical smear tests provide an early warning system for cancer of the cervix in women. Mammography, the technique for detecting breast cancers, is slowly reducing the number of deaths from breast cancer.

Cancer treatment

In general, surgery is used to remove the potentially deadly cancerous tumours. This is usually carried out in conjunction with other techniques. Radiotherapy, in which a beam of intense radiation is directed at the tumour to shrink or remove it altogether, is commonly used.

Chemotherapy is another common treatment. This involves the use of strong drugs designed to target the cancer cells. It can have many side effects, including nausea, hair loss and diarrhoea, because the drugs affect healthy cells as well.

On a broader front, certain antiviral drugs can help cancer sufferers. And in recent years, more potent anti-cancer drugs have become available. Some work by preventing certain growth factors reaching tumours; others prevent the cells from growing new blood vessels. Modern drugs are coming into use that attach themselves to cancer cells and kill them.

This woman is about to have a mammogram, in which X-rays screen for breast cancer or investigate lumps. Routine screening can detect tumours at an early and treatable stage.

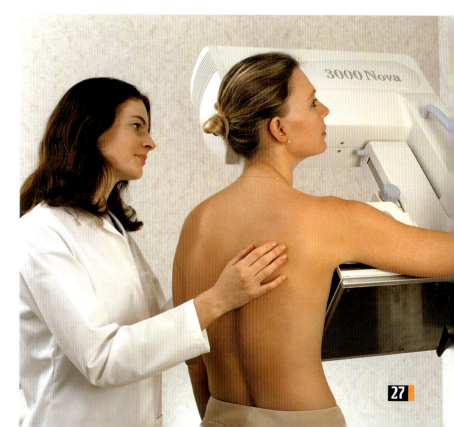

Complementary MEDICINE

From the earliest days of medicine, extracts from plants were used for healing. Plants are among the substances homeopaths use in their treatment. Homeopathy is one of a number of complementary medicines practised today alongside, or as an alternative to, mainstream medicine.

▲

This picture shows an aromatherapy massage. Essential plant oils massaged into the skin, in this case the jaw, are said to treat a range of disorders and conditions.

A German doctor named Samuel Hahnemann (1755-1843) invented homeopathy in the 1700s. He based it on his belief that 'like cures like'. For example, if you have a fever, a substance that would give you a fever if you were healthy should treat you.

A homeopath (a person who practises homeopathy) might recommend *Allium cepa* for hayfever. *A. cepa* is from the onion species; onions make the eyes water like hayfever. Hence it must be a suitable treatment for hayfever, which also makes the eyes water. In a similar way, *Rhus tox* (*toxicodendron*) is considered a treatment for itchy skin,

or eczema. It is the plant species poison ivy, which makes skin itch.

To be effective, homeopaths say, the plant extract has to be administered in minute quantities and is diluted many times in water. This procedure is called potentising.

Occasionally, some plant remedies hit the big time. In 1984, the German government approved the use of St John's wort as a natural anti-depressant. It was recommended as an alternative to prescription drugs like Prozac and quickly became a best seller. Millions around the world still take it regularly, even though its effectiveness has been questioned.

Getting the needle

Another popular complementary medicine is acupuncture, which has been practised in China for more than 5,000 years. The technique involves inserting fine needles into specific parts of the body.

The idea is that this treatment restores the balance of 'life energy', called chi, in the body. The acupuncturist taps into the meridians, or pathways, along which chi flows.

Acupuncture seems to work well on many patients. In China, it has even been used instead of anaesthetic in major surgery.

Massage and manipulation

The practice of shiatsu originated in Japan. Like acupuncture, it is based on improving the flow of chi through the body's meridians. The shiatsu therapist improves the flow by pressing on appropriate points along the meridians with the fingers.

Reflexology is also based on the idea of chi flowing through meridians. Reflexologists believe that various locations on the feet correspond to specific parts of the body. Tenderness in one part of the foot may indicate a blockage of chi in the pathway between the foot and the related body part, leading to illness. Touching and manipulating different parts of the feet clears the blockage, unlocks the chi and cures the illness.

Osteopathy and chiropractic are manipulative treatments that concentrate on the bones and joints, particularly in the spine. Releasing tensions in spinal muscles and tendons can help restore balance to the nervous system and improve the function of internal organs.

Aromatherapy is a treatment that uses essential oils derived from natural plant sources. These can be rubbed into the skin or inhaled. It is said to be particularly effective in relieving anxiety and depression.

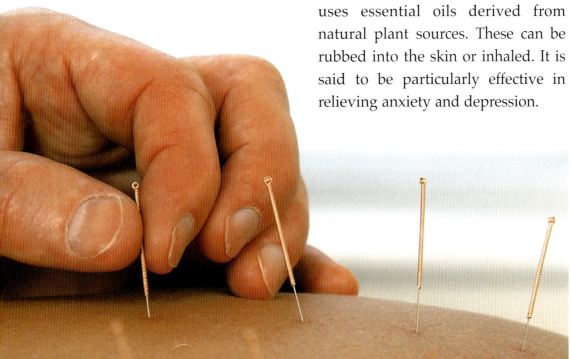

Acupuncture treatment involves fine needles being inserted into a patient's skin at specific points. It has been a part of Eastern medicine for thousands of years.

Tools of the TRADE

In the modern hospital, an increasing number of machines and devices are being used to diagnose medical conditions more accurately and to help in their treatment.

Since its invention in 1853, the hypodermic syringe is still the most common device used to inject drugs.

The stethoscope and sphygmomanometer are among the most useful devices. The stethoscope amplifies the sounds made by internal organs. The sphygmomanometer measures blood pressure.

Dating from the 1920s are the more recent electroencephalograph (EEC) and electrocardiograph (ECG). The EEC records and displays electrical activity going on in the brain. Abnormal EEC traces may indicate brain damage or disease.

The ECG records and displays the electrical rhythms of the heart. Irregularities in heart rhythms warn of probable heart conditions.

Life-savers

When a person does have a heart attack, the heart may stop beating. If this happens in hospital or in an ambulance, a machine called a defibrillator is used to try to get the heart going again. Via paddle-like electrodes, it sends an electric current into the chest to try to shock the heart back into action.

Kidney failure is another dangerous condition that machines

can deal with. Kidney dialysis machines remove dangerous toxic wastes that could threaten life.

Often called life-support machines, ventilators provide oxygen under pressure to patients who cannot breathe properly without assistance.

The scanning revolution

Imaging of the body began in 1895 when X-rays were first used to look at bones, and X-ray machines are still in use today. X-rays pass through the body and are recorded on photographic film. Bones show up because they block X-rays more than soft tissue does.

A more sophisticated X-ray technique, computerised tomography (CT), provides images of body tissues and organs in great detail. In a CT scanner, the patient is bombarded with X-rays from all directions. A computer converts the amount of X-rays the body absorbs in each direction into a series of 'slices', or cross-sections.

MRI and PET

MRI and PET scanners work on similar principles, but use different techniques. MRI (magnetic resonance imaging) scanners subject the body to radio pulses within a powerful magnetic field. Body atoms become excited and spin to align themselves with the field, giving off signals as they do so. A computer converts the signals into images.

In a PET (positron emission tomography) scan, the patient is injected with a radioactive substance. The machine records the radiation (particles called positrons) given off by body tissues, which a computer processes into images.

Ultrasound

Ultrasound scanning machines use high-pitched sound waves that are reflected from body tissues and organs. The reflections are picked up and converted into images.

Ultrasound machines are particularly useful for scanning pregnant women to check on the developing foetus because it would be too dangerous to use X-rays.

◄ ◄

A CT scan in progress. The screen in front of which the technician sits shows the body 'slice' being imaged.

▼

A pregnant woman undergoes an ultrasound scan. Ultrasound doesn't harm the developing foetus.

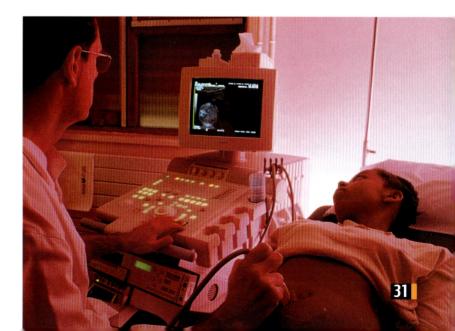

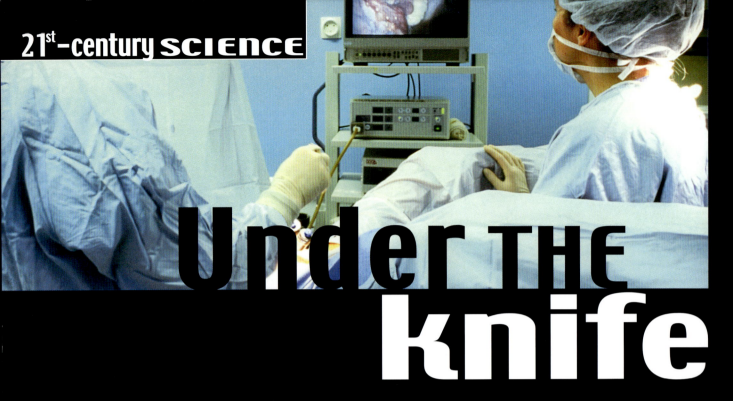

Under THE knife

Surgery plays a vital role in modern medicine, saving hundreds of thousands of lives a year. Open-heart surgery and organ transplants have become routine, while spare-part surgery is becoming more versatile. Keyhole techniques, which involve less invasive procedures, are growing in popularity.

▲

Keyhole surgery in progress. The surgeon is able to see what he is doing with the aid of a tiny camera in the endoscope.

Keyhole surgery

Keyhole surgery (properly called laparoscopy) is a rapidly expanding area. It is called keyhole surgery because it requires only tiny incisions (cuts) in the body. Many kinds of operations are now done using this technique, for example, knee surgery, abdominal surgery to repair hernias, and even surgery to remove tumours in organs like kidneys.

The essential tool used in keyhole surgery is the endoscope. This is a thin, flexible tube fitted with a light and a camera, which work through fibre-optic cables. The endoscope is inserted through a small incision to view the problem area. Miniature scalpels and other instruments can be passed along the tube to remove tissue if necessary.

Heart surgery

Several forms of heart surgery are carried out depending on what is wrong. Blocked arteries may be cleared by balloon angioplasty. A catheter (narrow tube) tipped with a balloon is threaded through an artery until it reaches the blocked vessel. The balloon is then inflated, compressing the deposit (plaque) coating the wall and opening up the vessel to allow a better flow of blood.

Often it is better to operate to bypass the blocked vessels. This is known as coronary artery bypass grafting, (CABG; also referred to as 'cabbage'). The surgeon does this by taking a vein from another part of the body and attaching it to either side of the blocked vessel so that the blood can take an alternative route. While the operation is underway, the heart is stopped and blood circulated by means of a pump called a heart-lung machine.

Transplants

If the heart is very badly damaged, the only solution may be to replace it with another healthy one. Heart transplants began in 1967 and are now carried out regularly. So are transplants of the kidney, liver and pancreas. Kidneys were the first organs transplanted, in the 1950s.

Surgically, transplanting organs is not too difficult. The real problem lies in the fact that the body tends to reject a new organ because the immune system perceives it as a foreign body. To combat this, patients have to take immunosuppressive drugs like cyclosporin. However, rejection is less likely to happen if the organ comes from a close relative.

Spare-part surgery

Another aspect of modern surgery is the increasing use of artificial parts to replace worn out, diseased or damaged parts of the body.

People have been fitted with artificial body parts, or prostheses, such as wooden legs and glass eyes, for centuries. In the modern world, a wide selection of artificial parts is available for internal and external use.

They include metal pins and plates to reinforce damaged bones; metal hip joints in plastic sockets; plastic blood vessels and silicone implants used in reconstructive surgery in breasts after cancerous tumours have been removed.

There are also more sophisticated devices like myoelectric arms, which work from electrical impulses from the wearer's own muscles.

The silicon chip may soon give some blind people the chance to see again. Experiments where light-sensitive chips are implanted into the retina have been encouraging.

Artificial hearts are being developed which may one day work well.

▼

A patient learms how to use a myoelectric arm after his own arm was amputated.

THE GENETIC revolution

In 1953, Francis Crick (1916–) and James Watson (1928–) made one of the most momentous discoveries of the 20th century. They determined the structure of DNA, the molecule of life. Fifty years later, international scientists finalised work on the human genome. Being able to find out what different genes do brings the prospect of successfully treating genetic diseases ever closer.

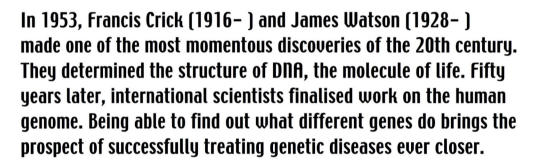

Genetics is the study of genes, the structures in cells that contain instructions to build and run the body, and pass on characteristics to future generations.

Genes are found in the central nucleus of cells. They are arranged along sets of long, thread-like molecules called chromosomes. There are 46 chromosomes (arranged in 23 pairs) in ordinary cells and just 23 unpaired chromosomes in sex cells (egg cells in females, sperm cells in males).

Looking at DNA

The molecule that forms the chromosomes and carries the genes is a chemical called DNA, or deoxyribonucleic acid. This has a remarkable spiral (double-helix) structure, rather like a twisted ladder. It is made up of two intertwining strands, linked by 'rungs'.

The strands consist of chains of sugar and phosphate units. The 'rungs' are made up of pairs of chemicals called bases. There are just four bases – adenine (A), thymine (T), guanine (G) and cytosine (C). To make the 'rungs', adenine always pairs with thymine, and guanine with cytosine.

A particular gene on a chromosome is represented by a segment of the DNA molecule and can be described by the sequence of bases along that section. Geneticists call each base (A, T, G, C) a letter. A set of three letters (for example, AGC, GTA) is called a word.

The human genome

The total set of genes that make up a human being is called the genome. In 1990, international teams of researchers began work on the Human Genome Project with the aim of identifying all the human genes and determining the complete sequence of letters (base pairs) in every strand of human DNA. The project was triumphantly completed early in 2003.

Before the project started, it was thought that humans had as many as 100,000 genes, but it was found that they have only about 30,000. But each gene consists of up to hundreds of thousands of letters, and the complete human genome has no fewer than 3,000 million letters.

When genes go wrong

Most people are born healthy and, provided they have adequate food and suitable living conditions, stay healthy for most of their lives. But some are born with a variety of disorders or diseases that they have inherited from their parents. The disorders originate mainly in their inherited genes.

Genetic abnormalities may be caused by the substitution of just a single letter in a gene. The runaway ageing disease progeria, which makes children die of old age by about 13, is a prime example. Other single-gene disorders include cystic fibrosis and sickle-cell anaemia.

Some genetic disorders are polygenic, which means they originate in more than one single gene. Examples are Alzheimer's disease, breast cancer and diabetes. Other genetic disorders can be traced to abnormal structures in the chromosomes, or even the presence of extra chromosomes, as in Down's syndrome.

The coloured DNA sequences that make up the pattern of the human genome represent years of genetic research.

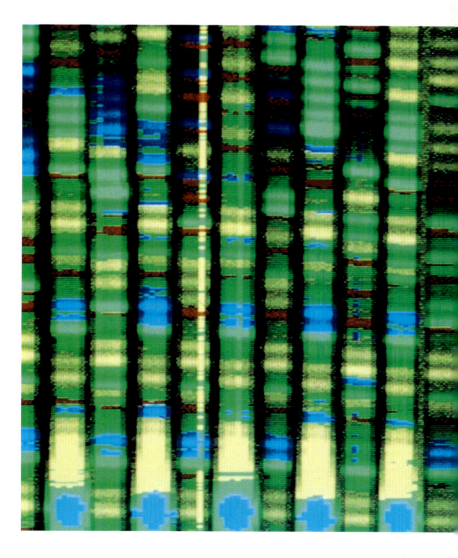

THE genetic revolution

Genes by number

The Human Genome Project has identified all the genes in the chromosomes of human beings. The chromosomes are usually numbered from 1 to 22 in order of their size. The 23rd pair includes the sex chromosomes – X and Y in males and two Xs in females.

Scientists already know what many of the genes on each chromosome do. They can also spot abnormalities in some of the genes, which may or may not cause a genetic disease. For example, abnormalities in a gene on chromosome 7 can cause cystic fibrosis. Certain genes on chromosomes 14 and 22 may bring on early-onset Alzheimer's disease. The presence of an extra copy of chromosome 21 leads to Down's syndrome.

Genetic screening

The greater understanding of DNA, genes and the work they do is leading to a revolution in the study of genetic disorders. Gene testing, or screening, is becoming widespread to identify people who may be at risk from inherited diseases, such as heart attacks or breast cancer.

Genetic screening will also reveal people who may not develop diseases but who may be carriers. For example, one in 300 people seems to be carrying cystic fibrosis.

Screening is often done on the foetus developing in the womb before birth. A common method is amniocentesis, which involves taking a sample of the amniotic fluid surrounding the foetus. This fluid contains cells shed by the foetus, which can be tested for defects, such as the extra chromosome that causes Down's syndrome.

Other techniques require DNA analysis, similar to genetic fingerprinting. The DNA is cut into fragments by so-called restriction enzymes. These fragments form a sequence called a DNA profile. This profile is unique to each person.

Genetic therapy

When faulty genes have been found, what can be done? The only permanent solution would be to replace them with normal genes.

Research into this so-called gene therapy is well advanced – for example, early trials on cystic fibrosis sufferers have proved promising.

In gene therapy, a carrier molecule, or vector, is needed to insert 'good' genes into the patient's cells to replace the defective ones. In current research, viruses are used as vectors because of the way they target cells. The virus is genetically altered to carry the good genes and to ensure that it is no longer harmful.

Genetic engineering

A technique of altering genes or transferring sets of genes between different organisms is called genetic engineering. It involves using chemical 'scissors' (restriction enzymes) to cut up the DNA of one organism into fragments, and then inserting a fragment into another organism. This technique is now widely used to engineer genetically modified (GM) organisms.

In medicine, it is being used to great advantage, for example, to produce insulin. The human insulin gene is introduced into bacteria, which then produce human insulin themselves. Among other genetically engineered medicines are growth hormone, blood-clotting factor VIII and a modified form of the hepatitis B virus for use as a vaccine.

▼

These E. coli bacteria have been genetically altered to produce human insulin. In this view, the insulin-producing parts of the bacteria are coloured orange.

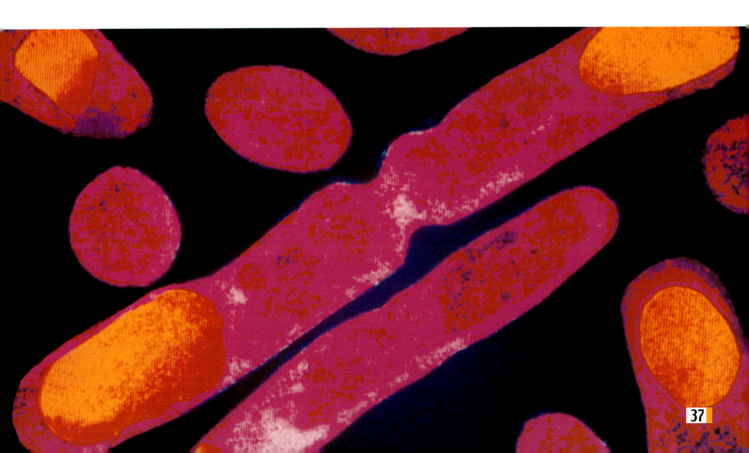

Life in VITRO

In July 1978, Louise Brown was born. She was the first 'test-tube' baby, who was conceived 'in vitro' – in a glass dish. Since then more than a million babies have been born by IVF (in-vitro fertilisation).

Many couples who want to have children find they cannot do so naturally, by sexual intercourse. Maybe the woman has a hormonal problem and cannot produce eggs, or maybe there is a problem with the man's sperm.

Fertility treatments and IVF

Doctors can improve a woman's fertility by giving her hormone drugs to improve egg production. This often stimulates several eggs to develop at the same time, which is a process called superovulation. If these eggs are subsequently fertilised, multiple births – twins or more – may result.

But fertility treatment by itself may not be enough, and this has led to the era of 'test-tube' babies. They are conceived by a technique known as in-vitro fertilisation, or IVF.

In IVF, eggs are removed from a woman who has been treated with hormones to bring about ovulation. The eggs are fertilised with a man's sperm in a laboratory in a glass dish. Then the fertilised eggs are transferred back into the woman's uterus a few days later.

By this time, the egg cells have divided to form four-cell 'pre-embryos'. If all goes well a baby, or babies, will be born.

Stem-cell research

Usually, a number of healthy fertilised embryos are left over after

IVF treatment. Some may be donated to treat other infertile couples, used for IVF research or destroyed.

More controversially, these excess embryos could be used in stem-cell research, which might lead to cures for disorders that currently defy treatment, such as Parkinson's disease.

Stem-cell techniques take embryos that are about a week old, when they have started to produce so-called stem cells. These are cells that, in a developing foetus, change into the many different kinds of specialist tissues that make up the various organs and systems of the body.

By removing these cells from the embryos and growing them in different conditions, scientists can theoretically convert them into specialist tissues, such as muscle cells or nerve cells. These tissues can then be used to replace diseased or damaged body tissues.

Cloning humans

Even more controversial is the possibility of human cloning, using techniques that have already produced cloned animals. The first successful animal-cloning experiments in 1996 famously produced a sheep called Dolly, who lived for more than six years.

Cloning would produce an exact genetic copy of another person. In cloning, the central nucleus would be taken out of human egg cells. Then these 'empty' cells would be mixed with ordinary cells from the donor, the person to be cloned.

A pulse of electricity or chemicals would fuse the two kinds of cells together, and some of them would start dividing and forming an embryo. The embryo would mature into a baby with genes that are identical to the donor's. He or she would be a clone.

◀ ◀

Born in summer 1996, Dolly the sheep was the first mammal to be cloned.

▼

A microscopic view of how cloning works. The nucleus of an egg cell is removed with a tiny pipette and replaced with a cell nucleus from the organism to be cloned.

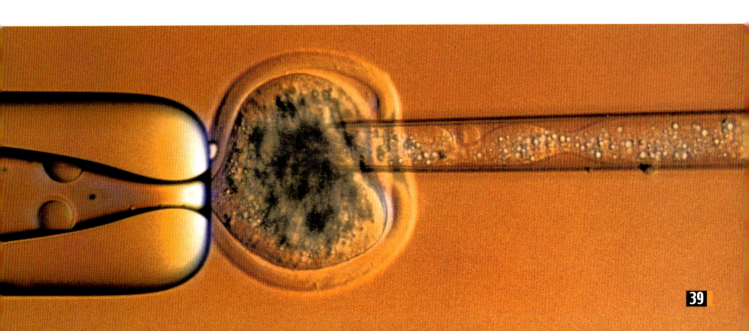

On the SPACE FRONTIER

Space medicine studies the effects of space flight on the human body. These effects do not prove serious for relatively short stays in space but could cause problems on long interplanetary journeys.

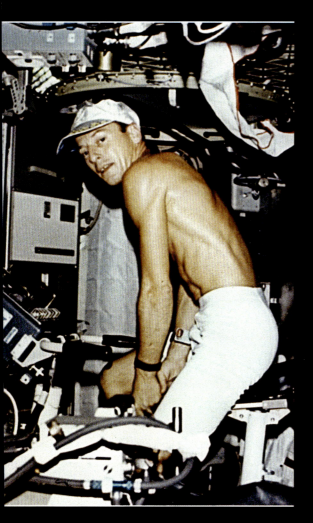

Research in space medicine, first begun in earnest on space station *Skylab* in 1973, now forms an essential part of work on the International Space Station. When astronauts fly into space, their bodies have a great deal to cope with. They withstand punishing G-forces at lift-off as the launch rocket accelerates into orbit, which makes their bodies feel up to 10 times heavier than usual. In orbit, they experience the peculiar state of microgravity, when gravity seems to have disappeared and their body appears weightless. On their return to Earth at the end of the mission, they must re-adjust to normal gravity.

The ravages of space

In March 1995, Russian cosmonaut Valery Polyakov returned to Earth after spending nearly 438 days in orbit in *Mir*. It was days before he could walk properly and months before his body returned to normal. Fourteen months in space had taken their toll.

But what exactly happens to the human body when it gets into space? The first effect most astronauts experience is a kind of travel sickness ('space adaptation syndrome'), but this usually passes in a few days.

Longer-lasting effects are caused by body fluids migrating upwards from the legs into the chest and head, giving astronauts puffy faces. The body starts excreting what it perceives to be excess liquid and gets rid of as much as one-fifth of total body fluid. This has little effect on the astronauts in space, but can make them feel weak and light-headed when they return to normal gravity on Earth.

Muscle and bone

More serious is muscle atrophy (weakening). Muscles in the arms and legs lose their strength because there is no gravity to fight against in orbit. Astronauts can lose up to one-fifth of their muscle strength after only a month in space.

More serious still is the condition called disuse osteoporosis, a deterioration of the bones due to calcium loss. Astronauts may lose as much as one-tenth of their bone mass on long flights.

Destination Mars

Will such space-based medical problems limit future human space exploration, such as flights to Mars? Even the briefest mission to the planet and back would take at least 18 months. Could the human body cope with such a journey? The answer is, probably.

Muscle loss on the outward flight could be minimised by exercise, with the astronauts working out regularly on bicycle machines and treadmills. Wearing special suits prior to landing on Mars would help them cope with the effects of Martian gravity. Bone loss should not be a problem, and might be minimised by special diet.

What about other hazards? Astronauts would need protection from deadly cosmic rays and from outbursts of radiation from the Sun. They might even need protection from Martian microbes. Recent evidence points to Mars once having had a wetter and warmer climate, in which primitive life forms like bacteria might have evolved.

Might some have survived and be dormant, waiting for a ride to another planet where they can thrive once more?

▲

A technician prepares medical tests aboard Spacelab, contained within the cargo bay of the space shuttle.

Astronaut Pete Conrad takes part in an early cardiovascular experiment on Skylab in 1973.

GLOSSARY

21st-century SCIENCE

antibiotic
A substance that kills bacteria.

antibody
A substance produced by the immune system to destroy invading organisms.

bacterium (plural bacteria)
A single-celled micro-organism that can cause diseases.

cancer
A disease in which body cells grow to form tumours (growths).

cell
The basic unit from which all living things are made.

chromosome
A structure within the nucleus (centre) of body cells that carries genetic material.

cloning
Producing a copy of an organism using the same genes.

CT (Computerised tomography)
A technique that uses X-rays to produce images of the body.

designer drug
A drug designed (usually with the help of a computer) to target a particular bacterium or virus.

DNA (Deoxyribonucleic acid)
A chemical found in every cell that carries instructions for growth and reproduction.

epidemic
The wide spread of a disease through the population.

gene
A unit found on a chromosome, which carries information about an individual.

genetic engineering
Altering the genetic make-up of a living thing.

genome
The complete set of genes that make up an organism.

hormone
A chemical that helps control body functions or behaviour.

42

immune system
The body system that helps protect it from infection.

immunisation
Injecting substances into the body to help protect it from invading organisms.

IVF (In-vitro fertilisation)
Fertilisation of eggs outside the body, usually in a glass ('vitro') dish.

keyhole surgery (laparoscopy)
Surgery carried out through a small incision.

micro-organism
An organism that can only be seen under a microscope.

MRI (Magnetic resonance imaging)
A body scanning technique that uses a powerful magnetic field.

organism
A living thing.

prosthesis
An artificial body part.

scanner
A machine that scans the body, producing images of internal structures.

space medicine
The study of how the human body is affected by space travel.

superbug
A bacterium that is resistant to antibiotics.

transplant
The replacement of a body organ by one donated from another person.

tumour
A cancerous growth caused by abnormal cell division.

ultrasound
Sound waves too high pitched to be heard; used in scanning.

vaccine
A substance injected into the body to stimulate its defences against diseases.

virus
A micro-organism that is on the borderline between living and non-living things.

X-rays
Radiation used in scanners and other machines to take images of structures inside the body.

21st-century SCIENCE

INDEX

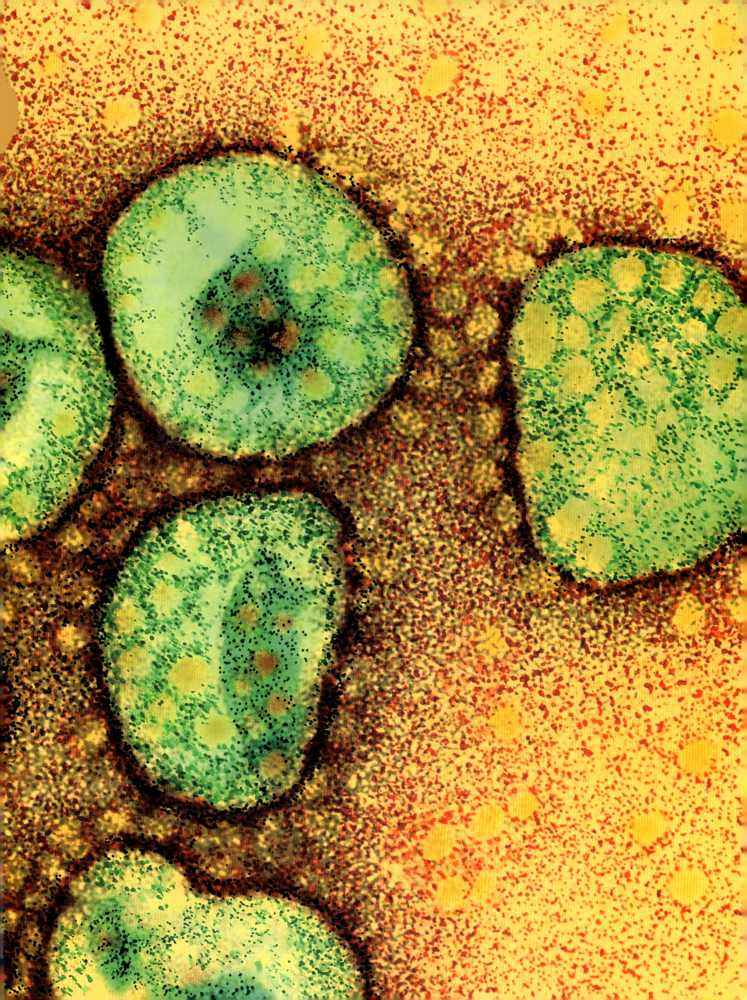

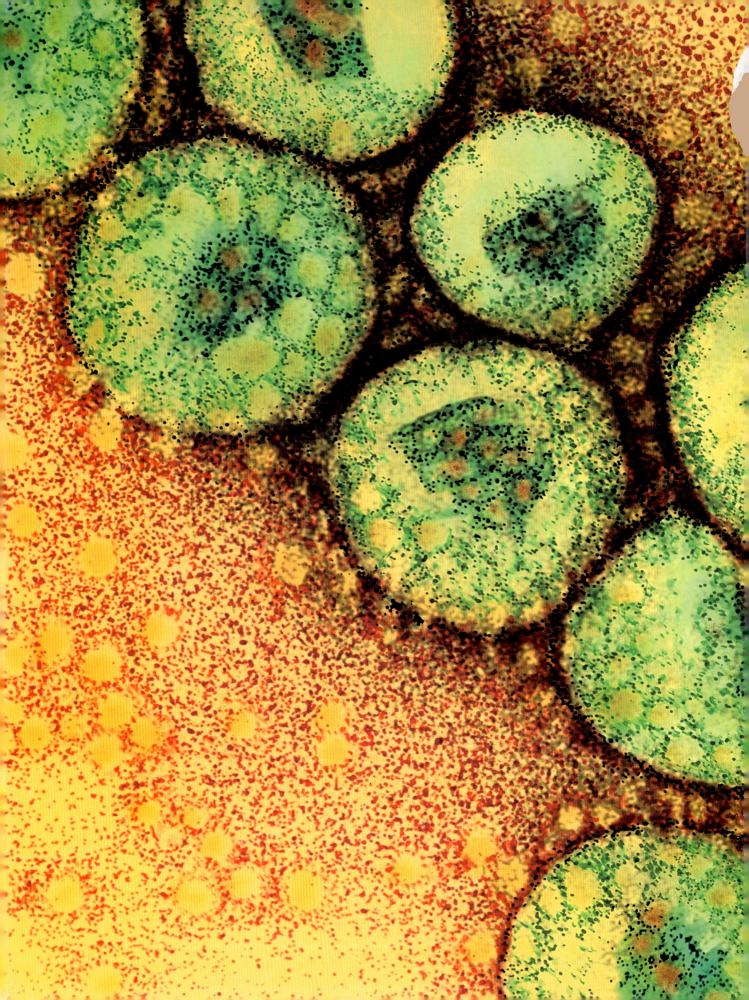